TOUCHING THE VOID

JOE SIMPSON

LEVEL 3

SCHOLASTIC

Adapted by: Rodney Smith
Fact Files by: Jacquie Bloese
Publisher: Jacquie Bloese
Editor: Patricia Reilly
Cover design: Dawn Wilson
Designer: Dawn Wilson
Picture research: Emma Bree

Photo credits:
Cover: Brand X/Punchstock. **Pages 4 & 5:** AFP/Getty Images; IFC Films/Everett/Rex; Allstar. **Pages 6 & 7:** S. Yates; J. Simpson; A. Cooper, D. Noton/Alamy; B. Glanzmann, P. Shermeister/Corbis; Allstar; Hemera. **Pages 8 & 9:** J. Simpson; Allstar. **Page 11:** Allstar.
Page 13: IFC Films/Everett/Rex. **Page 15:** S. Yates.
Pages 16–19: Allstar. **Page 20:** J. Simpson.
Pages 22 & 23: J. Simpson, S Yates. **Page 26:** AFP/Getty Images. **Pages 28–33:** AFP/Getty Images. **Page 34:** Allstar.
Page 36: J. Simpson. **Page 40:** AFP/Getty Images.
Page 43: J. Simpson. **Page 44:** Allstar. **Page 48:** D. Alderman/Alamy. **Page 53:** J. Simpson. **Page 55:** AFP/Getty Images. **Pages 56 & 57:** Allstar; BFI. **Pages 58 & 59:** M. E. McGrath/B. Coleman/Alamy; P. Bronstein, P. Parade/Getty images. **Pages 60 & 61:** LHB Photo, A. Ekins, Topdog Images/Alamy.

Illustrations: Hand Made Maps Ltd. (pages 4 & 5)

First published in the UK by Jonathan Cape, one of the publishers in the Random House Group.

Published by Scholastic Ltd 2007

Mary Glasgow Magazines (Scholastic Ltd.)
Euston House
24 Eversholt Street
London NW1 IDB

Printed in Singapore. Reprinted in 2009.
This edition printed in 2010.

Contents

JOE SIMPSON

Joe Simpson is a mountain climber from Sheffield, England. In 1985, he went to Peru to climb Siula Grande with his friend, Simon Yates. Joe's book, *Touching the Void,* is the true story of what happened to them during the climb.

SIMON YATES

Simon Yates also comes from the north of England. He has climbed all over the world.

RICHARD HAWKING

Joe and Simon met Richard, when he was travelling through South America. Richard stayed at their camp while they climbed Siula Grande.

SIULA GRANDE

Siula Grande is a mountain in the Cordillera Huayhuash, in Peru.

These mountains are in the centre of the country, about 250 kilometres north-east of Lima. Siula Grande is the second highest mountain, but it is the most difficult to climb.

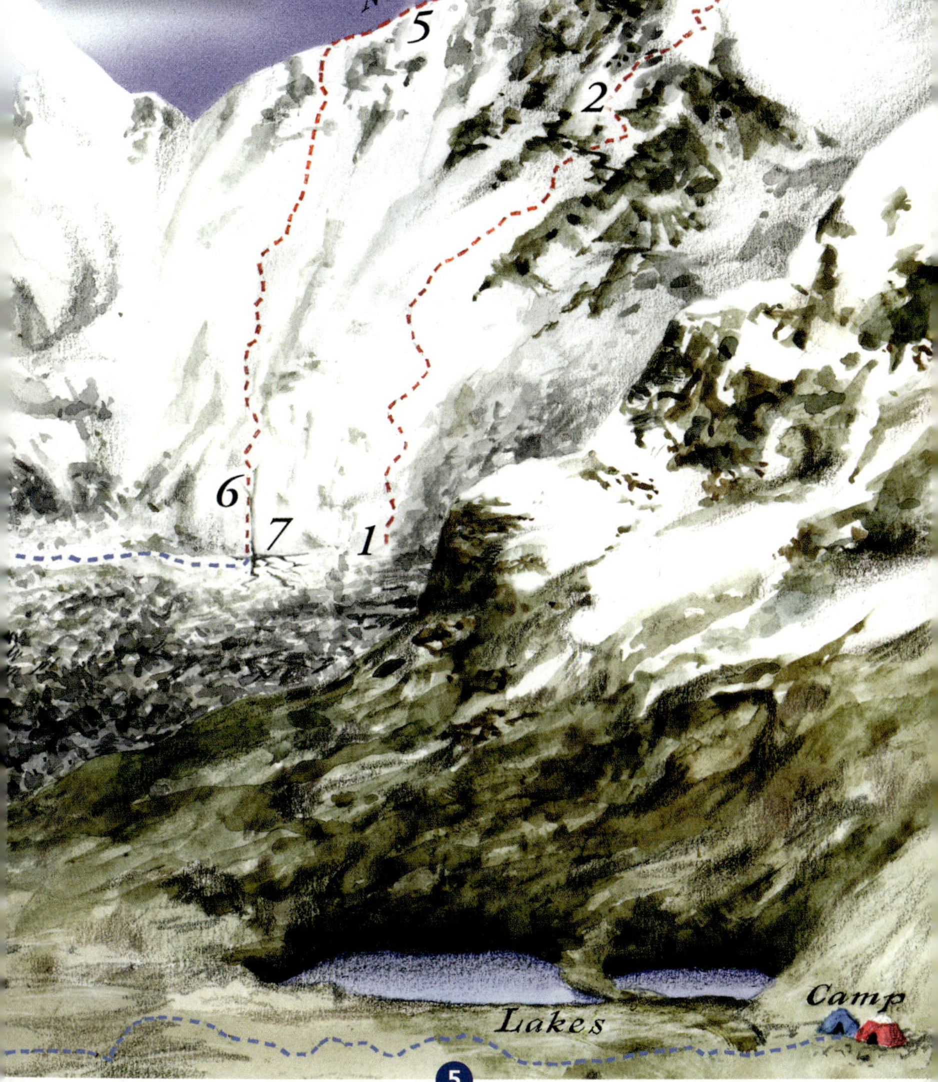

Mountains and

A glacier is a river of ice. It appears when snow from mountains is pushed together very hard.

A crevasse is a deep hole in the snow. It is not alway possible to see a crevasse, sometimes the entrance is covered with snow.

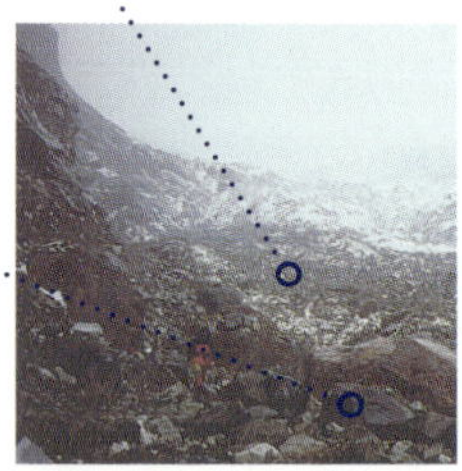

Moraines are the rocks and earth which are carried down and left by a glacier. They are often found at the sides of a glacier or below one.

A ridge is the long line where two slopes of a mountain meet.

Climbing

head torch
axe
helmet
bag
ice screw
harness
knot
sleeping bag
cooker
rope
gas
boots

TOUCHING THE VOID

CHAPTER 1
Getting ready

It was early morning. I was lying awake in my sleeping bag. My friend Simon was asleep beside me. We were in a tent in the Cordillera Huayhuash, high in the Peruvian Andes. We were about forty-five kilometres from the nearest village.

I got up. Outside, it was getting lighter. It had snowed in the night and the air was very cold. I walked to our cooking area and passed Richard's small tent on the way. Richard was a traveller who we had met in Lima. We both liked him. He told a lot of funny stories about all the interesting places he had visited around the world. We had asked him to join us and guard our things while we were away climbing.

I lit the gas on the little cooker to make a hot drink. As I waited for the water to heat, I looked at the mountains. I thought about why Simon and I were here. We wanted to climb the West Face of a mountain called Siula Grande. Nobody had climbed it before. We wanted to be the first.

I felt sure we could do it. We had both climbed difficult mountains in other parts of the world. We had sometimes had problems, but we had never had any serious accidents. However, as I looked at the mountains around me I felt a little worried. I knew this climb would be different. Siula Grande is 6344 metres high. It was much higher than any mountain we had climbed before. Our camp was at 4800 metres, which is as high as Mont Blanc in the Alps. The high, thin air would make climbing very tiring. Another danger was the weather. It could change suddenly. Large clouds from the Amazon could bring storms of snow, strong winds and terrible cold.

Later, during breakfast, I told Simon about my fears. He laughed. That was the good thing about Simon. He understood the danger, but it didn't stop him. He was the perfect climbing partner: optimistic, honest, and much less serious than me. He said the clouds didn't always bring storms and that worrying wouldn't help us. I agreed. I often wanted to be more like Simon.

We talked about the climb. We planned to do a few shorter climbs before Siula Grande for practice. Then we would spend two or three days eating and drinking to get strong for the climb.

We bought our food from a village family that Richard had met. There was Gloria, her sister Norma, and brother, Spinoza. Richard walked more slowly than Simon or myself and had taken longer to reach the mountains. He had met the family on the way up and spent a night with them. Now, they sold us all the food we needed.

During the next eight days we did three practice climbs. We didn't finish any of them because of the weather. While we were climbing, thick clouds would appear suddenly. They hid everything and climbing was dangerous. The snow was a problem, too. Sometimes it was too soft to walk on safely. Our second climb was the most interesting. It was on a mountain opposite our camp. As soon as we reached it, rocks started falling all around us like bombs. For this reason, I called the place 'Bomb Alley'. The rocks landed near a large wet boulder. Water ran over the boulder and there was a small pool below it. It was a good place to drink.

Our practice climbs hadn't been too successful, but we weren't worried. We had only done them to help prepare us for the main climb. Now it was time to eat, drink, and rest before we started our journey up the West Face of Siula Grande. For two days we ate and drank like hungry animals. By the end of the second day we felt strong and ready to go.

That evening I started worrying again. What if something went wrong? We could die. I told Simon. He laughed but I knew he felt the same. I also knew that a little fear was a good thing. It helped to prepare you. 'We can do it,' I told myself. 'We can do it.'

We had to wait another day because of bad weather, but the next morning was clear and sunny. It was time to begin the main climb.

We left camp. Richard was coming with us to the glacier which led to Siula Grande. Simon and I wanted to travel as light as possible so we hadn't brought our small tent. We would dig holes in the snow and sleep inside. That meant we only had to carry our climbing equipment and gas. We needed the gas to melt snow for drinking water. I thought two bottles of gas would be enough.

After an hour we came to an ice cliff. Richard could go no further. He took our photos. 'I could sell them if you don't come back,' he joked. We all laughed. I watched for a few moments as he started walking back to camp. I knew he would feel lonely while we were away.

Simon and I continued up the glacier. We stopped to put on our ropes and the rest of our climbing equipment. The sun shone brightly. The walls and fields of ice all around us shone like mirrors. It was beautiful, but climbing through the glacier was very hot and tiring. Every now and then we looked back. We wanted to remember the way we had come. Neither of us wanted to forget it on the way down. It was important to know if we should go below or above the crevasses when we returned.

By late afternoon we had reached the West Face of Siula Grande. We made a snow hole below the mountain and prepared for the night. 'Can we really do it?' I wondered as I lay in my sleeping bag.

Tomorrow we would know.

CHAPTER 2
A good start

The next morning it was very cold and my fingers ached badly. At first I couldn't use them but I knew they would be OK after I started climbing. I looked up at the mountain. It was bigger than I had thought.

'I'll go first,' said Simon.

There was no time to worry. I followed Simon up the first steep wall of ice. We climbed quickly in bright sun. We were joined together by 50 metres of rope. Every time Simon reached the end of the rope he put in an ice screw. He pulled to check it was strong enough. If it was OK, he called for me to climb up and join him. He sounded happy. I was, too. We were working well together.

By lunchtime we had climbed more than 660 metres to the top of the ice wall. We sat on a rock to have lunch. I felt pleased. In six hours we had climbed almost half way up the mountain. It was a great start.

I thought about what was ahead of us. I knew we had to find and climb a steep, narrow gully. At the top of this there was a second ice wall. This led to a wider gully. Here, we would dig a snow hole and rest for the night. We had about six hours to do all this.

Our first real problem came soon after lunch. We had to climb a little way across the West Face of the mountain to reach the narrow gully. The ice was thin and in places there was water under it. It was dangerous to climb and we had to move slowly. After a while, ice and small rocks started falling on us. I looked up. Huge ice cornices were hanging over our heads. If one of the cornices fell on us, we would be in serious trouble. We climbed faster and reached the narrow gully safely. It was 4.30 pm and in 90 minutes it would be dark. It was starting to snow.

We climbed the narrow gully quickly, but it took longer to climb the ice wall. It was very difficult at the top and again we had to move slowly. By this time it was getting dark. This made us both nervous.

Finally, we reached the wide gully and looked for some deep snow to dig a hole for the night. For a long time we couldn't find any snow that was deep enough. But then Simon found a huge hole in the snow. We made an entrance, cooked dinner and went to sleep.

It had been a good day.

CHAPTER 3
A difficult climb

Early the next morning I left the snow hole and looked at the mountain. I could see that it would be difficult to go straight up through the ice. Then I noticed an easier gully to the right. It seemed a better choice.

This time I was the leader. We started well and got to the top quickly. I had thought it would be easy to get to the top of the mountain from here, but I was wrong. The only way forward was through a strange wall of ice. Pieces of ice hung down. They looked like huge teeth. I broke some of the pieces with my axe and luckily I found stronger ice below. Quickly, I put in an ice screw.

We climbed onto another wide, open gully and stopped for lunch. The view was wonderful but it was much colder. There was nothing to protect us from the wind. From here, the way up to the top of the mountain looked even more difficult. We had to climb thin gullies between flutings of powder snow to reach it. Powder snow is very dangerous because it is too soft to put ice screws in. If we weren't careful, the snow could fall off the mountain. If that happened, we would fall with the snow. Also, some of the gullies were closed at the top. If we chose the wrong gully, we would have to climb over into another gully. That was always difficult. There was another problem, too. The weather was getting worse.

I led again. We were now climbing at a height of just over 6000 metres in cold, thin air. It was hard to breathe and we had to move slowly. When we reached the bottom of the flutings, a storm was coming towards us and it was beginning to get dark. We chose the widest gully. This time Simon went first.

The mountain was covered in thick cloud and it was snowing. There was also a very strong wind and the temperature was now about -20°C. It was almost impossible to see Simon above me. Ice and snow from his axe and boots fell on my head again and again. I was now extremely cold, tired, and thirsty.

We continued bravely through the storm, but by 10 pm we could go no further. We were both exhausted. It was the worst climb I had ever done.

We dug a snow hole, made a drink and ate the last of our food. We now only had one bottle of gas to melt snow. I was beginning to feel less optimistic. This climb was taking longer than we had hoped.

CHAPTER 4
At the summit

When we left the snow hole next morning, we saw that we were in a closed gully. We had to climb into an open gully to reach the top of the mountain.

I led, Simon followed. The storm had passed and the clear day made climbing easier. It also made me nervous: I could see all the way down to the bottom of the mountain.

Soon, we reached the top of the gully. This was the best place to cross to an open gully because the flutings were thinner. But which way should we go? Right or left? Simon told me to go right. It was the correct choice. I broke the walls of the fluting with my axe and crossed into the next gully. Simon joined me and then he went first.

As Simon climbed to the top of the gully, I suddenly became very nervous. I was standing on very soft snow and I could see all the way down to the bottom of the mountain. If the snow fell, then we would too.

I was very glad when Simon reached the top of the gully and climbed onto the North Ridge of the mountain. I joined him. At last we were off the West Face of Siula

Grande. We had successfully managed the most difficult climb of our lives. We now had a clear view of the summit. The way up was a steep, but easy, climb. But we were both very tired. We had done the most difficult part of the climb.

The climb up to the top of the mountain was very slow. We were now higher than we had ever been before in our lives and the air was very thin. When we reached the summit we stood and laughed. We took photographs and ate some chocolate. I felt pleased. I was also worried that climbing was becoming too important in my life. Every new adventure was more dangerous and I was worried about this. I always felt the same after reaching a summit. I was proud of my success. But the quiet moments after a difficult climb made me think about the future. I knew these feelings would pass.

'There's going to be another storm,' Simon said. I turned. He was looking at the North Ridge. Thick clouds were coming towards the east side of the mountain. I saw more flutings and steep walls of ice. This was the way down. Suddenly, I felt less confident. It didn't look easy. I was also worried because I knew that eighty per cent of accidents happen on the way down.

CHAPTER 5
Into a storm

It started to snow. We went towards the storm. Half an hour later we were climbing through the clouds and we couldn't see anything. I looked up and noticed the North Ridge through a hole in the clouds. We were below it, so Simon climbed back up to the top of the ridge.

Suddenly, both Simon and the ridge disappeared in a shower of snow and ice. The snow on the ridge had fallen. I was pulled into the mountain by the rope. Simon hung on the end of the rope on the other side of the ridge.

He managed to climb back up, but we were frightened. We knew that the ridge which we were walking on was very unsafe. We continued slowly. Soon, we noticed that the ground below us looked safer. We started to climb down again. It was 5 o'clock in the afternoon and the light was bad. The temperature was going down and the storm was blowing snow in our faces.

I thought that Simon was climbing too low. I shouted to him, but he couldn't hear me because of the storm. I shouted louder and Simon stopped. When I was climbing down to him, the snow suddenly disappeared under me. I fell and crashed into him. Luckily he didn't fall, and that saved us. It was very frightening.

'You okay?' Simon asked.

'Yes. Frightened … that's all,' I replied when I could speak again. 'We've gone too low.'

'Oh! I was thinking we could go all the way down to the glacier,' Simon said.

'You're joking!' I said. 'I nearly killed both of us on this bit. We have no idea what it's like below.'

'But that ridge is crazy. We'll never get down it tonight,'

Simon said.

We decided to go east in a straight line and join the ridge again further down. By the time it got dark we were still over 6000 metres. Neither of us felt very happy as we dug a snow hole. Simon had frostbite in two fingers. I hoped the frostbite wouldn't get worse the next day. I was sure that we were near the end of the ridge and that we would reach our camp by the afternoon. I hoped so – we only had enough gas for two drinks the next morning. And after that, there would be no more water until we got to the lakes.

CHAPTER 6
A terrible accident

The next morning we continued walking along the ridge. I was ahead of Simon. By now I was tired of the mountain. I just wanted to get down as quickly as possible.

Several times the snow disappeared under me and I fell into a crevasse. Luckily, none of the crevasses were very deep. But the falls were making me nervous. The last one was the worst. I fell through the snow and saw the whole of the West Face below me. 'How stupid,' I thought. 'I was walking on snow with nothing under it.' I shouted to Simon and told him to move to the safe side of the ridge.

I continued. I was feeling angrier and more upset every

minute. I walked over a small hill of snow. The ridge was flat again on the other side. I walked on for a few metres then stopped suddenly. I looked down. I was standing at the top of an ice cliff. The ridge was about ten metres below me. I turned round. Simon was behind the snow hill. I started climbing down the ice cliff. I used both my axes and tried to hit them hard into the wall. I was still near the top of the cliff when one of the axes made a strange noise. I pulled it out of the cliff. Then I lifted my arm to hit again. Suddenly, the other axe came out of the ice and I fell. A moment later my knee crashed into the ice wall and I screamed in pain.

The pain seemed to last for a long time. 'If I've broken my leg, I'm dead,' I thought. Everyone said it … if there are only two of you, a broken leg can mean death. When the pain was less I tried to move my leg and screamed again. It was no good: I had broken it.

I looked around. We were still at about 6000 metres and I wouldn't be able to climb with a broken leg. Simon would leave me. He had no choice. I thought about it. Left here? Alone? I felt cold at the idea. I wanted to scream, but I knew I had to stay calm.

Joe disappeared behind a pile of snow in the ridge. A few moments later the rope went loose. It meant that Joe had stopped. I waited. I was glad to rest. When the rope moved again I continued walking. Suddenly the rope went tight and I was pulled forward. I hit my axes into the snow and managed to stop. I knew that Joe had fallen. I waited. When the rope went loose again I knew Joe's weight wasn't on it. I walked forward to see what had happened.

I reached the edge of the ice cliff and looked down. Joe told me calmly that he had broken his leg. There was a terrible look in his eyes. I didn't want to think about what this accident meant. I put a metal bar in the snow and tied the rope around it. Then I climbed down to Joe. I could see that his leg was badly broken. I gave him some pills for the pain, but I don't think they helped much. At this time, my thoughts were selfish. I knew it would be easier to walk away and try to save myself. I tried to pull the rope down. It wouldn't come. I had to climb back up the cliff and get it. The climb to the top of the cliff was the most dangerous climb I had ever done. I almost fell several times. But at least I stopped thinking about Joe's accident.

I reached the top of the cliff and untied the rope. I was surprised when I looked back down the cliff. Joe was climbing down a slope, away from the cliff. He was hopping slowly on his good leg and I could see that he was in great pain. I knew then that I could never leave Joe while he was fighting so bravely. I would do everything I could to get us both down the mountain.

CHAPTER 7
Getting down the mountain

Simon and I decided to tie our two ropes together. That gave us 100 metres of rope. Simon would dig a hole in the snow. Then, he would sit in the hole and lower me down.

Our plan worked very well. We quickly went down 100 metres but it was now four o'clock and another storm was coming. We had two choices: we could dig a snow hole for the night or we could continue down the mountain. We decided to continue down.

Simon was lowering me very fast in a terrible storm. I was in great pain because my knee kept hitting the side of the mountain. I felt angry that he was hurting me, but I knew he had no choice. We had to get down quickly.

By 7.30 that evening we knew we were getting close to the bottom of the mountain. It was now completely dark and the storm was very bad. I knew we should stop, dig a snow hole and melt some snow for water. But we couldn't because we had no gas.

Just then, I felt the slope getting steeper. I realised that there was another cliff. I screamed to Simon to stop lowering me. He couldn't hear me, because the wind was too loud. Suddenly, the side of the mountain disappeared under me and I fell into space.

The rope pulled against my body and I stopped. I had gone over a steep ice cliff and I was hanging about 26 metres above a black crevasse. I tried to reach the walls of the cliff with my axe. They were too far away. I knew my weight would soon pull Simon off the mountain. When that happened, we would both die. I had to get back up the rope and I had to do it quickly. My only chance was to use two smaller pieces of rope that I had with me. I could tie these small ropes around the main rope with special knots. Then I could use them to climb to the top of the main rope.

My fingers were so cold that I couldn't feel them. It took fifteen minutes just to tie one knot. Then I dropped the other piece of rope. At that point I knew there was nothing more I could do. I hung on the end of the rope and waited to die. I knew the cold would soon kill me.

CHAPTER 8
Falling

I felt quite pleased after three and a half hours of lowering Joe down the mountain. The storm was very bad and my hands were terribly cold. My frostbite was worse. But I knew we were close to the bottom of the mountain. Suddenly, I noticed more weight on the rope. I thought Joe was just going over steeper ground. I continued lowering him to the end of the rope. I pulled the rope. This was the sign for Joe to take his weight off the rope. But nothing happened. I waited and still nothing happened. Then I knew that I had lowered Joe over an ice cliff. He couldn't take his weight off the rope. He was hanging in space.

I stayed there for an hour and a half and tried to think of something I could do. But things just got worse. I was shaking with cold and Joe's weight was slowly pulling me off the mountain. Suddenly I started to move. I dug my feet into the snow again, but I knew that it was useless. In a few minutes, we would both die.

Then I remembered the knife in my bag. I decided quickly. I would have to cut the rope. I didn't have a choice. Carefully I took the knife from the top of my bag and cut the rope.

I started to fall and screamed. Seconds later, I landed on ice and snow in a cold dark place. I didn't know what had happened. I just knew that I wasn't dead. I realised that I was lying on an ice bridge inside the crevasse. I knew then that I was lucky to be alive.

The bridge wasn't flat and I started moving. Quickly, I put in an ice screw. The rope was hanging through the hole above me. I was sure that Simon was lying dead on the other end. I pulled the rope. I thought it would soon go tight from the weight of Simon's body. But it didn't.

It just kept coming. Finally, the other end of the rope dropped through the hole and fell on me. I saw then that it had been cut. 'You are going to die in here,' I thought, but I was also pleased that Simon was alive.

I felt very alone and very frightened. I could hear strange noises all around me. I hated the dark so I turned on my head torch and looked around. I couldn't see any way out.

'What a terrible place to die,' I thought. I was young, healthy, and I had dreams for the future. Now, I would die in a cold, dark hole at the bottom of a mountain. Why had I ever come to Siula Grande?

'Stupid,' I screamed. 'Stupid, stupid, stupid.'

Some time after I cut the rope, I dug a snow hole and tried to sleep. I couldn't. I couldn't stop thinking about Joe. I hoped he might still be alive, but I knew that was almost impossible. It was a long night. I was afraid and terribly thirsty.

I looked at my watch. It was 5 am, I had been asleep. I knew Simon was somewhere above me so I called his name over and over again. The hours went by and there was never any answer. I knew then that I was completely alone.

CHAPTER 9
The way out

As soon as it was light I collected my equipment and left the snow hole. By this time I was sure that Joe was dead. I thought that I was going to die, too. It seemed fair. However, I didn't want to just wait for death. I would keep moving while I could.

Soon the ground below me dropped steeply. I climbed down and saw an ice cliff over a crevasse. 'So that's what Joe went over!' I thought. But the most awful thing was the crevasse. Joe had fallen into that deep dark hole. The idea was terrible. I felt guilty. I knew that if I hadn't cut the rope, I would be dead. But still I felt guilty. I had survived. Now I was going home, but I would have to tell people what had happened. Who would believe it? Nobody cuts the rope! 'Why didn't you do this?' 'Why didn't you try that?' I could imagine the questions.

I climbed down the cliff and looked into the crevasse. I didn't have enough rope to climb down inside.

'JOE!' I shouted but there was no answer.

I wasn't surprised. He was dead.

When I finally reached the glacier I was still sure I was going to die. Glaciers are dangerous. There are deep crevasses everywhere. You can't see them because they are covered in snow. You might fall through and die any moment. However, I was lucky. I managed to cross the glacier safely.

I had to decide. I couldn't just stay where I was, waiting to die. I had to lower myself down the crevasse. It was the only way. I didn't know how deep it was. I only had about 26 metres of rope. If it was very deep, I would reach the end of the rope. Then I would fall and die. But I had to take the chance. Slowly, I started lowering myself down.

By the time I reached the end of the glacier I could hardly stand. I was very tired and thirsty. I found some water on the moraines and had a long drink. But I was feeling bad about Joe. How could I explain what had happened to his parents and my friends?

'You killed him.' They might not say it, but they would think it.

I thought about lying. I could just say that Joe had a terrible accident.

Just then, I saw Richard. He looked worried. When he saw me he was surprised and happy.

'Simon! It's good to see you. I was worried,' he cried.

I couldn't speak. Richard started looking around for Joe. Perhaps my face told him something terrible had happened.

'Where's Joe?' he asked.

'Joe's dead,' I said.

'Dead?' he said.

I sat down, silent.

'You look terrible!' Richard said. 'Did Joe fall? What happened?'

'Yeah, he fell,' I said. 'There was nothing I could do.'

Richard gave me some hot tea and chocolate. Then he passed me the medicine bag.

I told him exactly what had happened. I couldn't do anything else. Richard listened in silence. I was glad I was telling him the truth. I couldn't lie. When I finished Richard looked at me.

'I knew something terrible had happened. I'm just glad you managed to get down,' he said. He understood. He didn't think I had done the wrong thing.

We walked quietly down to the camp. Richard prepared a hot meal. For hours I slept in the hot sun, then we ate again. I was still exhausted. Slowly I felt my body becoming stronger again. That evening there was another storm. We lay side by side in the tent listening to the storm. It was very, very cold outside. Finally I fell into an exhausted sleep.

After about 25 metres my feet touched some ice. Opposite me, I saw light through a hole in the roof. There was a slope up to the hole. Suddenly everything seemed better. This was the way out that I had hoped to find. The only problem was the ice that I was standing on. It wasn't the bottom of the crevasse. It was very thin and there was nothing under it. I could fall through at any time.

I crawled slowly across the ice on my stomach. I was very nervous. I could hear things falling under me. I tried not to think about the thin ice. After a few minutes I reached the other side. The ice was harder now and I felt safer.

I looked up at the light which was coming through the hole in the roof. 'This is it,' I thought. 'This is the way out.'

I used my good leg to climb up the slope. I used the rope to help me. I still felt a lot of pain but slowly the hole got closer.

It took over five hours to reach the hole in the roof. Finally I pushed my head out of the hole. It was a bright, sunny day. The whole world had returned. I was alive. I pushed myself out of the hole and lay on the snow. For a few moments, the heavy weight of pain and fear seemed to lift.

CHAPTER 10
Crossing the glacier

I was happy. I had escaped from the crevasse. But when I looked around I felt less confident. I saw the huge glacier and thought, 'You haven't even started yet.'

I could see there were still a lot of problems ahead of me. I had a broken leg and frostbite in both my hands. I didn't have any food or water. How could I survive a journey of almost ten kilometres over dangerous ground to our camp?

Slowly, I managed to hop to the glacier, but how would I cross it? Then I saw Simon's footprints in the snow. I knew that I would be safe if I followed them. I thought about the best way to move. I couldn't hop, so I lay on my left side. Then I hit both my axes into the snow. Finally, I used the axes to pull myself along the ground. I tried not to think of the kilometres between me and our camp. It was just too far. I had to break the problem into smaller pieces. 'I must reach that wave of snow over there in twenty minutes,' I thought. Slowly and painfully, I started moving forward. I didn't think about reaching the camp. I only thought about reaching the place. Then I chose the next place and moved forward again. I did this again and again. From time to time I stopped to eat snow and rest.

I was soon moving forward quite well. As I crossed the glacier I heard two voices in my head. The first voice was strong and sensible. It told me to forget the pain and keep moving. The only important thing was to reach the next place I had chosen. The second voice understood how I felt. 'Rest for a while, your leg hurts,' it would say. I tried not to listen to the suggestions of the second voice. Only the first voice would help me to survive.

For a long time I followed Simon's footprints. The journey was like a game. I chose a place. If I reached it in less than twenty minutes, then I passed the test. This made me extremely happy. If it took me longer, I failed. Then I felt angry and upset.

Everything was going quite well until it started to snow. This was a serious problem. I realised that the snow would soon hide Simon's footprints. I became extremely worried. I tried to move forward as fast as I could.

I felt I was losing the race. It was getting dark and the temperature was going down. I followed the footprints until I could see no more. It was dark. I lay down in the snow. I only wanted to sleep but the wind kept waking me. And then the voice screamed inside my head. 'Don't sleep. Don't sleep, not here. Keep going. Find a slope and dig a snow hole … don't sleep.'

I kept moving through the dark. I had no idea where I was going. Suddenly, I fell down a steep slope. I couldn't stop and I landed at the bottom of a huge pile of snow. It was time to stop. I crawled back up the snow and found a place to dig a hole for the night. I don't know how I managed to dig. I was extremely tired and thirsty and the pain in my knee was terrible. It took me a long time to get into my sleeping bag. I lay down and looked at my watch. It was ten-thirty. I had crawled over the snow with no food or water and a badly broken leg for more than twelve hours.

I knew I had to sleep, but I couldn't. I was safe, but pain and worry kept me awake. I was worried that if I fell asleep I might not wake up. For a long time I lay in the dark with my eyes open.

Finally, I closed my eyes and fell into a black, silent sleep.

CHAPTER 11
The end of the glacier

It was late when I woke up and the sun was shining through the tent. I felt very strange. It was only thirty-six hours since I had left Joe, but it felt like weeks. I felt completely empty inside. Joe was gone and there was nothing I could do to change it.

I had breakfast with Richard but I said very little. Then I walked up to the lake, took off my clothes and jumped into the water. I washed myself and my clothes. Then I shaved in the warm sun and I started to feel better. I had cut the rope and Joe had died. I felt guilty, but his death wasn't my fault. I had done everything possible to save him. Other people might not agree. But, for the moment, I didn't feel so guilty any more.

I walked back to camp. Richard had gone for a wash. I looked around the tent for the medicine box and found it under a pile of Joe's clothes. I threw everything out the door of the tent and went outside. I took some pills for my frostbite, and then I started to look through Joe's things.

I made two piles: the things I would give his parents and the things I would burn. I found his diary, but I didn't want to read it. I would give it to his parents. I also found a hat he liked. I decided to give that to his parents, too.

When Richard returned we took Joe's clothes to the river bed and burnt them. We returned to camp and sat and played cards or listened to music.

The deep, empty feeling inside me refused to go.

I woke up screaming. I had dreamt that I was still inside the crevasse. In the dream I was lying on the snow bridge. My head was against a wall of ice and I was crying. It was all so real that I believed I was still in the crevasse. I soon remembered where I really was. I sat up, broke a hole in the snow roof and felt warm sunshine. I was still alive and it was going to be a hot day.

There was no sign of Simon's footprints. The snow had completely covered them. I knew the moraines were in front of me but I couldn't see them. All I could see were waves and waves of fresh snow.

As I collected my things together I was feeling terribly thirsty. I had had no food and very little water for two days and three nights. Yesterday had been bad. I thought today would be impossible without any water. I would die of thirst before I reached camp. But I knew I must at least try. Sitting on the glacier and worrying wouldn't help.

I started to crawl away from the snow hole. I was still doing the same thing. I gave myself a time to get to the next place. After an hour, I got onto my good leg and stood up. I could see the beginning of the moraines. They weren't too far away but I still had to cross several crevasses.

At one point, I had the idea that perhaps my right leg wasn't badly broken. I decided to try and stand on both legs. As soon as I put weight on my right leg I felt a terrible pain and crashed to the ground.

Walking was impossible, so I had to continue crawling. This meant that I couldn't see the way through the crevasses. I lay on my back. I didn't want to move. Then the voice came back: 'Don't lie there. Get up. Keep moving.'

Slowly I started crawling forward.

From time to time I had to stand up to see where I was. The moraines didn't seem to be any closer. I felt like I was moving from side to side. I kept going although I felt completely lost.

Time seemed to stand still as I crawled across the crevasses.

Finally, I lay down on a snow bridge between two crevasses. I was exhausted. I felt unable to continue. 'Is this the end?' I thought. But as I looked around I realised something.

'I know this place,' I thought. I could see that the bridge turned to the left and then dropped down. There was only one way to find out what was beyond that. Slowly and in great pain, I stood up. There was a huge dark boulder at the end of the bridge. I was safely through the glacier and I had reached the beginning of the moraines.

CHAPTER 12
Looking for water

I was very happy after getting through the crevasses safely. But, as I looked down the moraines towards the lake I discovered that I couldn't see very well. There was something wrong with my eyes. Nothing I looked at had clear edges any more. 'Oh no! That's the last thing I need,' I thought. I knew what had happened. I had lost my sunglasses and I had had to look at the bright white snow for many days. This had hurt my eyes. Luckily, I was now on the moraines and there was less snow. I hoped that my eyes would get better.

I lay against a rock. It was warm in the sun and I went to sleep. I woke to the sound of the voice in my head: 'Come on. Wake up. There's still a long way to go.' I looked at my watch. I had been asleep for half an hour.

I left most of my climbing equipment by the rock so that I didn't have to carry it. I also decided to tear my sleeping mat in half and tie it around my bad knee. I had to use the axe to cut it. I tied the mat around my knee as tight as I could and stood up.

The rocks lay ahead of me like a hard brown river. I knew I wouldn't be able to crawl. Walking was impossible, too. The only thing I could do was hop on my good leg. I needed a tall stick to help me to stand, but I didn't have one. I only had my axe. It was very short, but it was all I had. It would have to be good enough.

After my first hop I crashed to the ground in great pain. I kept trying until every second hop was just about OK. Slowly the hopping got better. I was falling less and less.

I started down the moraines at one o'clock. I had five and a half hours before it got dark. I needed water and I knew there was water in Bomb Alley. I didn't think I could get there before dark, but I had to try.

I fell many times and sometimes I cried with the pain. The voice inside my head kept saying: 'Put the axe on a rock, lift your foot forward, hop ... axe-lift-hop ... keep going. Look how far you've gone. Just do it, don't think about it.' I forgot why I was doing it. I just kept repeating the actions. I did the same as before when I was crawling through the snow. I chose a place and gave myself a time to reach it.

After two hours I looked back at the glacier. It was now just a dirty white cliff far away. I was doing well and felt

happy. I only listened to the voice in my head and tried to forget everything else. Pain and feeling thirsty were the only two things that I couldn't completely forget. Even these were less important than my watch and the voice. I only failed to reach the place I had chosen once. I lay by the rock it had taken too long to reach. I cried in anger.

There was no sign of life in the moraines: no birds, no animals, nothing. I could hear the sound of water under the rocks, but I couldn't reach it. My world was pain and water. It was making me a little crazy, but there was nothing I could do.

Finally, I found a little water. A thin line of water ran down a large rock and landed in the wet earth. I drank the water from the ground. I couldn't drink much because it was mixed with a lot of dirt and small stones.

The weather was good all afternoon. The skies were clear and I knew that there wouldn't be a storm that night.

I saw that the ground ahead of me suddenly sloped down. I knew that I was reaching the ice cliff at the end of the moraines. This was where Richard had said goodbye to us on the day we started the climb.

Soon, I reached the cliff. It wasn't as steep as the cliffs higher up. I started going down. When I was half way down, the rock that I was holding moved. I fell down to the bottom of the cliff. Luckily, I fell against a large rock and didn't fall any further. I was in pain, but nothing worse.

I looked back at Siula Grande. I had got down the mountain. I had crossed the glacier and hopped down the moraines. I felt I had won some kind of fight. I smiled and thought: 'Maybe I can even reach Bomb Alley before tonight.'

That was my big mistake. I had suddenly become too confident. I stopped listening to the voice. I only thought of Bomb Alley and the water there.

I forgot about choosing the next place to reach. I stopped checking my watch. I just moved forward as darkness slowly came.

I got lost in the dark. I was falling more often and it was getting more and more difficult to stand up. I had been too optimistic. Then, the voice came back. 'This is stupid. Stop and get into the sleeping bag.'

This time, I listened to the voice.

CHAPTER 13
Bomb Alley

Except for the frostbite in my fingers, my body felt healthy. But I still felt empty inside. Richard was worried about me. He thought we should return to Lima as soon as possible. The idea was sensible, but I just couldn't leave immediately. I looked at the mountains. They were holding me there, refusing to let me go.

'I think we should leave.' Richard spoke suddenly.

'What? … It's just … I'm not ready …' I said.

'Look,' he said softly, 'Joe's not coming back. You know it. I know you'd go back if there was a chance, but there isn't.'

'Perhaps you could go on ahead. I can follow later,' I suggested.

'Why? Come down with me. It'll be better that way,' he replied.

I didn't answer.

'I'm going down to see Spinoza,' Richard continued. 'We'll need to borrow his mules for the journey. He'll agree if we pay him enough.'

'OK,' I agreed. 'But let's stay here just one more night. We can go in the morning.'

'Yeah, OK,' he replied. 'See you soon.' As I watched him go I still felt uncertain.

Richard returned two hours later and told me that Spinoza would be there early the next morning. I felt happier now that we had decided. I also remembered some money I had hidden in the rocks before the climb. We looked around the camp, but couldn't find it. We needed the money to pay Spinoza so we started searching near our cooking area. A few minutes later I found my money bag under a rock.

As it got dark that night, I felt a few drops of rain. The rain soon turned to snow and we went inside the tent. Another storm was coming. We closed the tent door and cooked the evening meal inside.

We played cards for a while. Then we turned off the light and got into our sleeping bags. Outside, the snow fell. It covered everything with its cold, silent whiteness. I thought of the snow falling on the glacier below Siula Grande. The awful ache of emptiness returned.

The sun rose and started to warm me. I didn't want to move. I could feel that I had got worse in the night. I didn't feel strong enough to continue. My life depended on finding water. Without water I was finished. If I could get water, I would have a chance. I knew if I didn't reach the camp that day then I never would.

Suddenly I had a terrible thought. 'Will Simon and Richard still be at the camp?' Perhaps they had gone. Simon had been back for two days. He would be stronger now. There was no need to stay at the camp.

The thought made me sit up. I had to continue. I must reach camp today. I looked at my watch. It was eight o'clock. I had ten hours.

It took a long time for me to stand up. After the first hop I crashed to the ground. I stood up again and held on to a boulder. I tried another hop. My foot didn't leave the ground and I fell on my side in great pain. This time the pain didn't go. I couldn't go on. I was finished.

The voice saved me. It came back, stronger than ever. 'Keep going. You can't stop now.' The voice made me realise how far I had come. It would be stupid to die here, after coming so far. The thought made me angry.

I started hopping forward and soon fell again. When I landed on the ground, my face felt wet. I heard the sound of water running over rocks. I realised I had reached Bomb Alley.

For a long time, I drank and drank. Finally I stood up. I was feeling strong again. Once again, I started moving forward.

Hours passed. I lost all feeling of time. Reaching the next place and the voice were the only important things. I noticed that the boulders were now mixed with smaller rocks. Sometime in the afternoon I checked my watch. It was three o'clock. Ahead of me was a steep gully which went down to the lake. I had reached the end of the moraines.

CHAPTER 14
Cries in the night

I crawled down the gully and by four o'clock I had reached the lake. I knew that the lake became narrow at the far end. Here, there were some rocks. On the other side of the rocks there was a smaller lake. At the end of the smaller lake there was a wall of rocks and dirt. The camp was just below it.

I had to sit facing the mountains and move backwards along the side of the lake. I was feeling extremely tired again, but I listened to the voice and kept moving.

Two hours later I reached the second smaller lake. By now, I was feeling terribly weak. The idea that Simon and Richard had left the camp came back and filled me with fear. The weather was getting worse again, too. Huge clouds were moving down from the mountains. Moments later, the sun disappeared. I kept moving until I reached the wall at the end of the second lake. I stood up just as it started to rain.

I hit my axe into the rocky wall and jumped forward with my good leg. The wall wasn't very high but it took a long time to reach the top. From there I looked down towards the camp.

I couldn't see the camp. The whole valley was filled with clouds which hid everything. I moved slowly down the far side of the wall. It was almost dark now and it was snowing. Had Simon and Richard gone? I just didn't know.

'Si – m – on,' I called. 'SIIIIMMMOOONNNNN!' I waited. There was no answer.

I lay against a boulder. I was feeling terrible. I was completely exhausted. I was colder and weaker than I had ever been. And I was lost. Which way should I go? I had no idea.

I moved forward into wind, cold and darkness. Hours went by and my head was full of strange thoughts. A song I didn't like came into my head. It was mixed with pictures from my past. I heard the sound of people laughing, screaming and crying. I wanted to turn off these mad thoughts and sleep. But the voice was still there. 'Don't,' it cried.

By now, I was sleeping, waking, crawling and sleeping again. I didn't think I would survive. Once, I realised that I was on the dry floor of the river, but then I fell asleep. When I woke I had forgotten again.

Sometime during all this, the voice disappeared. I had nothing to keep me going any longer. I was going to fall asleep. I knew if I fell asleep I might not wake up again, but I was too tired to fight. It was a bad smell that stopped me falling asleep.

When I smelt it, I suddenly woke up completely. I knew where I was. I was sitting in the toilet area of the camp. The smell was awful, but I was too tired to move any more. I could only shout.

'SIIIIIMMMMMmmmooonnnn....' I cried, as loud as I could. 'Please be there. You must be there. Come on! Help me please. Help me.'

Snow hit my face, the wind pulled my clothes, and the night stayed black. Warm tears ran down my face.

'HELP Meeeeeeee.....'

The night ate my words. Simon and Richard had gone. There was nothing left.

Suddenly, I saw coloured lights moving through the darkness. What were they? Was I imagining things that weren't there? I saw a brighter light.

'The tents!! They're still here …' I thought.

Then I heard voices. They were coming closer.

'Joe. Is that you? JOE?'

It was Simon. I tried to shout back but nothing came out. I started crying and fell to the ground.

'Over there, over there!' I heard the shouts.

Seconds later, I was covered in light.

'Help me … please help.'

I felt strong arms around my shoulders, pulling me. Suddenly I could see Simon's face.

'Joe? Oh my God!' Simon called out to Richard. 'Help me! Lift him!' Together they carried me into the tent.

'It's OK. I've got you. You're safe,' Simon said.

Simon and Richard carried me into the tent. They fed me and gave me cups of hot tea. There was too much to say, too much to explain. That could all be done later. Except for one thing.

I looked at Simon. 'Thank you. You did the right thing.'

Simon nodded silently.

'Thank you,' I said again. I knew I could never thank him enough. He turned away.

'I've burnt your clothes,' he said.

'What?' I was surprised.

'Well, I thought you weren't …'

Simon laughed at the look on my face. Then we all laughed. I was back. I was with friends.

CHAPTER 15
Journey to Lima

I was alive, but Simon was very worried about my leg. It wasn't straight. It was fatter and covered in large areas of yellow and purple.

'You've got frostbite and your leg looks really bad. We have to get you out of here,' he said.

'But I need rest and food. I can't do a two-day journey by mule now.'

'Well, you'll just have to,' said Simon. He had decided and I couldn't refuse.

'Simon?' There was something else, something very important I had to say.

'What?'

'You saved my life. You got me down the mountain. We were just very unlucky with that last ice cliff. It must have been terrible for you after you cut the rope. You did the right thing. You had no choice. I understand that. I just want to thank you for saving me.'

Simon turned away. There were tears in his eyes.

I felt tears filling my eyes, too. Seconds later, I was asleep.

In the morning, Gloria, Norma and Spinoza arrived with the mules. I waited while Richard and Simon tried to agree with Spinoza about the price. It took a long time.

Our idea was to go to the nearest town, Cajatambo. From there we would take a bus to Lima.

We were about to go when I remembered a money bag I had hidden before the climb. There were more than two hundred dollars in it and we needed the money. I called out instructions to Simon and Richard and they finally found it under a rock. Now we were ready to go.

The next two days were a cloud of pain and tiredness. Sometimes I felt that I was getting worse, not better. I was extremely weak. I was frightened. The strong, calm voice had gone. Without the voice, I was alone. I felt that I could still die on the journey.

At Cajatambo we paid the driver of a truck to take us to Lima. We agreed to take an old man with us because both his legs were broken.

The journey took three days. The driver spent most of

the time smoking cigarettes and drinking beer. I did, too. Simon also gave me pills for the pain in my leg.

At the hospital the doctors looked at my leg. They told me I needed an operation quickly. But nothing was quick in Lima. For two days I had to lie in a hospital bed without food. Finally, they took me into the operating room.

Suddenly, I wanted to stop the operation. I wanted to wait until I was back in England. I tried to sit up. 'Please. Don't …' I said. I was pushed back down. I felt something going into my arm. I watched the bright lights above me slowly disappear. Soon they were lost in darkness and silence.

CHAPTER 16
Remembering Siula Grande

Since climbing Siula Grande, many people have talked about Simon cutting the rope. Some of these people have said it was the wrong thing to do. Climbers should always stay together. Other people have said that Simon made the right choice. 'Why,' they ask, 'should someone die for no good reason?'

Simon and I both know he did the right thing. He had tried bravely to get me down the mountain. In the end, Simon saved my life. I will always be grateful for that.

TOUCHING THE VOID:

Joe Simpson's amazing story, *Touching the Void*, was first published in 1988. It caught the interest of people all over the world – including several film-makers. At one time, Tom Cruise's film company were interested in making the film – with Tom Cruise as Joe Simpson! Then, British director Kevin MacDonald read the book. 'I loved it,' he said. 'This isn't just a story about climbing. It's about life itself. I knew we had to make the film.'

Return to Siula Grande

Most of the climbing action in *Touching the Void* was filmed in the Alps with actors. However, Kevin Macdonald's plan was to film the second part of the film on Siula Grande. He wanted to film a reconstruction with Joe.

In 2002, Joe Simpson and Simon Yates returned to Siula Grande in Peru with the film crew. Joe felt very nervous. 'I feel strange about coming back,' he said. 'Since the climb in 1985, I've been very lucky in my life. A part of me feels that the good luck might end because I'm back here again …'

First, the crew made the long journey from Lima to Siula Grande. Then they set up camp where Joe and Simon had camped seventeen years earlier. Here, Joe and Simon met Richard Hawking again. They hadn't seen or spoken to Richard since 1985. 'We thought you were dead!' Simon joked.

When the crew were more comfortable with the thin air at the camp, they moved up to the glacier. Here, at the bottom of Siula Grande, they started filming. Joe had to pretend to have a broken leg and crawl and hop across the glacier. The reconstructions took several days, and Joe didn't enjoy the time. 'Seventeen years ago, I lost everything in this place and then I got it all back. I don't want to remember feeling like that.'

Have you seen any 'docudrama' films like *Touching the Void?* Do you like them? Why/Why not?

'Filming was hard for everyone because of the cold and the thin air,' Kevin Macdonald remembers. 'But Joe and Simon had to live through the whole thing again, which was extremely difficult for them.'

The film

The film came out in 2003 and won several awards, including 'Best British Film'. *Touching the Void* is a 'docudrama' – a mix of a documentary and a film. It mixes interviews with Joe, Simon and Richard with filmed action. The result was very successful. Joe was happy with the final film but said, 'For me and Simon, nothing can begin to describe what happened to us.'

What do these words mean? You can use a dictionary.

publish crew reconstruction award documentary interview

making the film

Joe and Kevin talk during the filming

Climbing Everest

Reporter: Why climb Everest?

George Mallory: Because it's there!!

Tenzing at the summit

What do these words mean? You can use a dictionary.

gods base adjust altitude icefall zone

In 1852, it was decided that Mount Everest, in the Himalayas, was the world's highest mountain. And ever since then, men and women have wanted to climb it! Many try, a few are successful and some lose their lives …

Mallory and Irvine

British climbers George Mallory and Andrew Irvine tried to reach the top of Everest in 1924. They had already tried twice. Sadly, they disappeared. Nobody knows if they ever reached the summit.

Hillary and Tenzing

In 1953, New Zealander Edmund Hillary and Sherpa Norgay Tenzing became the first people to reach the top of Everest. They had simple equipment and no ropes. When they reached the summit, Tenzing put sweets in the snow for the gods. They stayed there for only 15 minutes before going back down. Hillary and Tenzing became famous all over the world.

The way to the top

Everest is over 8000 m high. There are five camps, including 'Base Camp', before reaching the summit.

Base Camp is at 5000 m. Climbers usually spend two weeks here to adjust to the altitude. During that time, Sherpas set up ropes in the dangerous icefall above. Many climbers and Sherpas have died here – killed by falling ice.

After Camp IV (7900 m), climbers enter the 'Death Zone'. They can't stay here for more than two to three days because of the altitude. If the weather isn't good enough to continue, they have to go back down to Base Camp.

It takes ten to twelve hours from Camp IV to reach the summit. Climbers usually spend less than 30 minutes at the summit because they need to be back at Camp IV before dark.

Why do you think people want to climb mountains like Everest? Would you like to try it?

Who are the Sherpas?

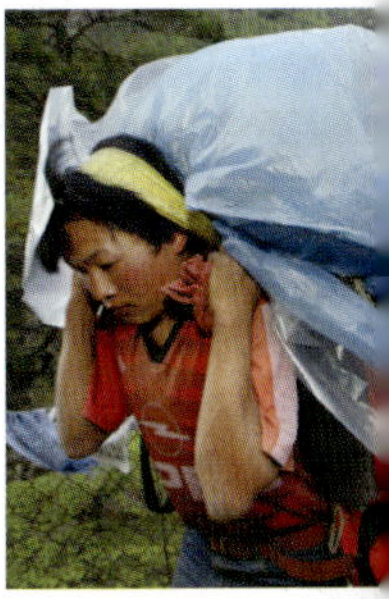

The Sherpa people come from the mountains in Nepal, high up in the Himalayas. Many Sherpas helped the first climbers who came to Everest. They carried equipment and worked as mountain guides. Today, the word 'sherpa' is used for any guide or helper in the Himalayas.

EVEREST FACTS

- About 1500 people have reached the summit
- Junko Tabei from Japan was the first woman to reach the summit in 1975
- Over 200 people have died on Mount Everest since 1922
- Everest is growing by 4-10 cms every year

"I want to be

Do you love being outside in the countryside, coast and mountains? Did you climb up trees, walls or other things when you were younger? Do you want to try a sport that tests your intelligence as well as your strength? Then, climbing could be for you …

A climbing wall

Where do I start climbing?

'Climbing walls' in climbing centres are great places to start. They can be inside or outside. There, you can go to climbing classes.

What do you learn on the climbing wall?

First you will learn 'bouldering'. This is the simplest technique – you don't use ropes and you don't go up very high. You can also try this on boulders outside. You need a mat to jump on to.

After bouldering, you will learn how to climb with ropes. The climber wears a harness and a rope. Their partner controls the rope from above. Then, if the climber falls, it won't be far.

Would you like to go climbing? If 'yes', what do you think you would enjoy most? If not, what kind of sport would you like to try?

Later, you can try 'lead-climbing'. Here, your partner controls the rope from below. As this is more dangerous, both climbers need to be experienced. Joe Simpson and Simon Yates used this technique when they climbed Siula Grande.

What equipment do I need?

You will need special climbing boots, ropes, a harness and a helmet. You can borrow these from a climbing centre.

When can I start climbing outside?

This depends on your skills as a climber. Climbing outside is more difficult than inside climbing for many reasons. For example, climbing walls have coloured 'holds' to show you where to climb; rocks do not have these! Start with easy climbs.

When climbing outside, you must go with an experienced climber, or a climbing group.

a climber!"

When is the best time of year to go climbing?

You can climb at any time of year and in almost any weather. If you're learning to climb, try to climb in good weather.

Where should I go on my first outside climb?

Get a climbing guide book and choose a climb that suits your skills. Don't just choose any rock – it may be unsafe. Bits could fall off and hurt you. In the UK, the Peak District in the north of England, and Snowdonia in Wales are popular places to go.

TOP CLIMBING TIPS

- Never climb alone. Always go with an experienced climber or climbers.
- Make sure that you always have the correct equipment with you.
- Look after the environment. Be careful with your equipment on the rocks and don't leave anything behind.
- Remember – climbing can be dangerous. People die every year in climbing accidents. Think about you and your partner or group's safety at all times.
- Enjoy it!

What do these words mean? You can use a dictionary.

strength control experienced harness technique helmet environment

CHAPTERS 1 – 5

Before you read
You can use your dictionary for these questions.

1 Complete the sentences with these words.
axe rope boulder camp alley frostbite glacier
- **a)** You can tie a ... to a person or thing.
- **b)** You can use an ... to cut things.
- **c)** A ... has tents to sleep in.
- **d)** A ... is made of ice. It moves very very slowly.
- **e)** You get ... when your skin gets very cold. Your skin goes black.
- **f)** A ... is a big rock.
- **g)** An ... is narrow. It has walls on both sides.

2 Choose the correct word.
- **a)** Go to bed, John. You look exhausted / melted.
- **b)** I'm tired of winter. I want the snow to dig / melt.
- **c)** Help me dig / exhaust this hole. I want to plant a tree.

3 Choose the best ending.
- **a)** If a job is tiring,
  - **i)** you probably want to rest.
  - **ii)** you probably want to continue.
- **b)** If there is a void,
  - **i)** there is an empty space.
  - **ii)** there isn't any space.
- **c)** If there's a bomb in the shop,
  - **i)** you leave quickly.
  - **ii)** you stay and look around.

4 Look at the map on pages 4-5. Do you think it will be easy to climb this mountain? Why / Why not?

After you read

5 Answer the questions.
- **a)** Why does Joe want to be more like Simon?
- **b)** Why was the second practice climb the most interesting?
- **c)** What was Simon and Joe's first real problem?

d) Why is powder snow dangerous?
e) What does Joe worry about at the top of the mountain?
f) What happens to Simon after he climbs to the top of the ridge?

6 What do you think?
a) Why is Joe nervous after the storm?
b) Who is the most optimistic, Simon or Joe? How do you know?
c) Why are Simon and Joe not happy at the end of the third day?

CHAPTERS 6 – 10

Before you read

You can use your dictionary for these questions.

7 Complete the sentences with these words.
slope hop lower knot head torch guilty crawl
a) If you want to join ropes together you have to tie a … .
b) A … helps climbers see in the dark.
c) I did something wrong. Now I feel … .
d) A baby can …. on its hands and legs before it can walk.
e) We were higher after walking up the … .
f) I could only use one leg so I had to …. across the room.
g) The cat can't get out of the tree. I'll use a rope to … it down.

8 Match the two halves of the sentences about climbing.
a) It is more dangerous
b) Climbers need gas
c) An axe is used
i) to break ice.
ii) to go down a mountain.
iii) to melt snow for water.

9 What kinds of accidents could happen when climbing?

After you read

10 Correct the sentences.
a) When Simon looked back down the ice cliff Joe was waiting for him.
b) When the storm came Simon stopped lowering Joe.

   c) After falling, Joe managed to reach the walls of the cliff with his axe.
   d) Joe fell to the bottom of the crevasse.
   e) Richard thought Joe was wrong to cut the rope.
   f) Joe hopped across the glacier.

11 Have you ever felt very frightened or been in danger? Did you feel at all like Joe? What happened?

CHAPTERS 11 – 16

Before you read

12 Answer the questions.
   a) What three mistakes did Simon or Joe make when they climbed Siula Grande?
   b) What do you think will happen at the end of the book?

After you read

13 Answer the questions.
   a) What problem did Joe have when he was crawling across the glacier?
   b) What was Joe's 'big mistake' after he reached the end of the moraines?
   c) Why does Simon feel so bad about cutting the rope?
   d) Why does Richard want Simon to leave the camp?
   e) What was Joe's biggest worry after he reached the second lake?

14 What do you think?
   a) Why did Joe Simpson decide to write *Touching the Void*, do you think?
   b) If you were Simon, would you cut the rope?